I0440921

SAMMY MEETS A STAR!

By: Shirley Priscilla Johnson

Dedicated To:

Danny
Jamie
Paulette

Always keep Sammy in your heart and the memory that these stories bring of childhood smiles and family love.

I LOVE YOU!

MOM

Sammy had had a busy day, watching the children as they played.
Now the night had settled in, but sleep for, Sammy, was far from him.

Sammy looked and saw a startling sight.
Right up above him he saw
      a light!
He knew the sun had gone to bed.
It wasn't the moon, for that was
      way overhead.

Sammy thought it might be a plane.
But.............it did not move.
So.....he thought again!

Perhaps I'll float up a little higher
I can't get to sleep so it might be
worth while.

Sammy went up, went up some more.
This light was really high, that's for
sure.

Finally Sammy was face to face, with a light that had such a Heavenly face. The light was so bright it hurt Sammy's eyes, so he put on his sunglasses and turned and said, "Hi!"

"I saw your light," Sammy said, "What is your name and what do you do? My name is, Sammy, and I've never seen you."

The light seemed to chuckle and said,
"I'm a star. I come out at night and
brighten the sky. There are many of us,
if you will look you will see. We're lights
for the night, my brothers and me."

Sammy said, "Oh, I see what you do. You light up the sky, you and the moon. You do at night what the sun does at day. Now I'm awful tired, so I'll be on my way."

Sammy floated back down and closed his eyes. Seems he learns something new as each day goes by.

THE END!

S AMMY MEETS TABYA!

By: Shirley Priscilla Johnson

A RAINY DAY STORY JUST FOR

YOU!

Sammy had only been a cloud for maybe a week or two. He'd only met Mr. Sun, and been in a sky of blue.

Sammy didn't understand why it wasn't getting light. Instead of the sky being bright and blue, it was almost as dark as night!

Soon the children came out to play,
but when they looked at the sky – one
by one they went back in their house –
and Sammy wondered why!

Sammy floated here and there, not knowing what to do, and than he came upon a cloud that had the darkest hue. Sammy turned and said, "Hello, what kind of cloud are you? And could you please tell me why today the sky's not blue?"

The cloud did not say anything, just floated right on by. Then Sammy saw him meet a friend, and another way up high!

Now Sammy thought and pondered this. He knew an answer must be there. He was just about to give up hope when another cloud appeared.

The cloud said, "Hello, my name is, Tabya. What are you doing here? You're a fluffy, sunny day cloud, the kind that watches the children play, why are you here today?"

My name is, Sammy, and yes, I always watch the children play. But I don't understand where the blue sky is, or why the sun has gone away.

"Sammy," said Tabya. "Today is a rainy day. The earth needs water to give life so the children have a place to play. Because of rain, the flowers grow, and the grass becomes green for the children, you know."

Oh, Sammy thought. Now he understood that this was Tabya's day, to give the earth a drink so the children had a place to play.

Sammy floated off, but knew he'd be back again. He waved at, Tabya, who he knew would be his friend.

Thank you for sharing Sammy with us. If you would like Sammy on DVD, please go to our website for information. Here you will find other children's stories and some great stuff for mom and dad too.

Remember, Sammy is always ready
To play.

www.funport.com/insong/default.htm

Please be on the lookout for more "Sammy The Cloud," adventures coming your way.....

Published by: Createspace
A Division of Amazon
www.createspace.com

www.ingramcontent.com/pod-product-compliance
Lightning Source LLC
Chambersburg PA
CBHW050932290526
45792CB00002B/986